What is Jewish Thinking?

UNDERSTANDING THE CLASSICAL
WORLDVIEW OF THE BIBLE AND RABBINIC
THOUGHT

Juan Marcos Bejarano Gutierrez

Yaron Publishing
Grand Prairie, Texas

Copyright © 2019 by Juan Marcos Bejarano-Gutierrez.

All rights reserved. No part of this publication may be reproduced, distributed or transmitted in any form or by any means, including photocopying, recording, or other electronic or mechanical methods, without the prior written permission of the publisher, except in the case of brief quotations embodied in critical reviews and certain other noncommercial uses permitted by copyright law. For permission requests, write to the publisher, addressed "Attention: Permissions Coordinator," at the address below.

Juan Marcos Bejarano-Gutierrez /Yaron Publishing
701 Forest Park Place
Grand Prairie/Texas 75052
www.CryptoJewishEducation.com

Book Layout ©2017 BookDesignTemplates.com

Ordering Information:
Quantity sales. Special discounts are available on quantity purchases by corporations, associations, and others. For details, contact the "Special Sales Department" at the address above.

What is Jewish Thinking?/ Juan Marcos Bejarano-Gutierrez. —1st ed.
ISBN 9781686629273

Contents

Preface 6

Jewish Thinking 9

    Jewish Thinking as a Type of Thinking 11

Jewish Thinking and Hellenistic Thought 18

    Greek and Hebraic Sources of Knowledge 23

    Syllogistic Thinking versus Juxtaposition 26

Polarity in Jewish Thought 29

    Polarity as the Pillar of Jewish Theology 30

    Polarity in Biblical Literature 32

    The Problem of Evil 34

    The Nature of Man 36

    Polarity as Essential to All Things 38

The Rabbinic Mind 41

    Logical Thinking in Rabbinic Thought 47

Thinking about Judaism in Non-Jewish Ways 53

Christianity and Greek Thinking 67

Yehuda Halevi and Moses ben Maimon 79

    Yehuda HaLevi's Views 80

    The Views of Maimonides 85

Accommodation or Particularistic Approaches 93

The Particularistic Approach 94

The Accomodationist Approach 98

Saadia Gaon: The First Medieval Accomodationists 100

The Accomodationists of Medieval Spain 103

The Accomodationist Position in the Medieval Period .. 105

18th Century Accomodationism 107

Am I an Accomodationist or Particularistic? 112

Index 121

To my beautiful wife, who supports all my academic endeavors.

"A woman of valor, who can find?"

Rabbi Simcha Bunam of Przsycha (a Hasidic Rebbe of the 4th generation after the Baal Shem Tob) gave the following definition of a *Hasid*. A *Hasid* is a person that goes beyond the letter of the law. The Torah in Leviticus 25:17 states:

וְלֹא תוֹנוּ אִישׁ אֶת-עֲמִיתוֹ, וְיָרֵאתָ מֵאֱלֹהֶיךָ: כִּי אֲנִי יְהוָה, אֱלֹהֵיכֶם.

This can be translated as follows:

"And ye shall not wrong one another or Thou shalt not deceive thy fellow-man… but thou shalt fear thy God; for I am the LORD your God. "

A Hasid, according to Rabbi Bunam, goes beyond the letter of the law; he will not even deceive his own self.[1]

---

[1] Abraham Joshua Heschel, *God in Search of Man: A Philosophy of Judaism* (New York: Farrar, Straus, and Giroux, 1983), 11.

Preface

In the year 167 BCE, a small band of Judean priests sparked a conflict against the Seleucid Empire that would last a quarter of a century. The immediate trigger had been a sacrifice to idols about to be offered by a Jew at Seleucid officials' order. The battle was not merely a violent reaction against foreign rule, however.

The violence that erupted also revealed the profound disagreements between Jews over what Jewish identity entailed and how it should be lived out. While the military battles against the Seleucid Empire that followed were momentous, the heart of the clash was religious.

Hellenism had spread throughout the Near East. It encompassed polytheistic ideas that quickly absorbed other cultural beliefs and religions. The Seleucids had no issues with Jews as a people. Judaism was monotheistic, and this presented a problem. Their problem was the unwillingness of many Jews to change their understanding of Judaism. Hence, the real war was one of ideas.

The Judean rebels known as the Maccabees were ultimately successful in creating an independent Jewish state which lasted almost a century. As much as their struggle sought to return Judea to previous periods of Jewish spiritual and political autonomy, the Hasmonean rulers were themselves influenced by Greek thought, language, lifestyle, and education.

Despite this, a commitment to the Hebrew Bible prevented many Jews from embracing Hellenism completely. The Hebrew Bible formed the basis from which classical Judaism developed. Understanding Jewish thought based on the Hebrew Bible and later rabbinic writings help explain the uniqueness of the classical Jewish worldview, which continues to this day.

The original edition was titled *Against the Greeks*. Since its initial release, I have added two complete chapters and have revised some other material. I hope this new title better encapsulates the theme of this book.

CHAPTER 1

Jewish Thinking

Blaise Pascal was a well-known scientist of the 17th century. I first learned about him in elementary school because of his famous mechanical adding machine. Lesser known to me were his philosophical and theological endeavors. At the time of his death, a note was found in his pocket. It read "the God of Abraham, the God of Isaac, the God of Jacob, and not the God of the philosophers."

This simple but profound statement encapsulates the assertion that fundamental differences exist between the God of Israel described in the Bible and the Supreme Being envisioned by Western philosophy. Professor

Michael Wyschogrod comments on Pascal's specific designation:

> "The matter of God's name is of no small importance here. The God of Israel has chosen to hyphenate his name with the people of Israel. He is identified as the God of Abraham, Isaac, and Jacob. After all, what other name could he go by…the only viable name is the 'God of Abraham, Isaac, and Jacob,' tying God's identity to the people of Israel. It is as the God of this people that he becomes known by all the people of the earth. To such an extent does God permit his identity to be intertwined with that of the people of Israel." [1]

---

[1] Michael Wyschogrod, *The Body of Faith: God and the People of Israel* (Northvale: Aaronson, 1996), 11. Abraham Joshua Heschel provides another reflection on the identification of God with the people of Israel: "The term 'God of Abraham, Isaac, and Jacob' is semantically different from a term such as 'the God of truth, goodness and beauty.' Abraham, Isaac, and Jacob do not signify ideas, principles or abstract values. Nor do they stand for teachers or thinkers, and the term is not be understood like that of 'the God of Kant, Hegel, and Schelling.' Abraham, Isaac, and Jacob are not principles to be comprehended but lives to be continued. The life of him who joins the covenant of Abraham continues the life of Abraham. For the present is not part of the past. 'Abraham is still standing before

It is important to note that Pascal was a devout Christian and the rest of his statement elaborates on the centrality of Jesus' redemptive role in the Christian faith. For our purposes, Pascal's argument is nevertheless revealing since he specifically targeted the western philosophical tradition and its image of the Divine. Western philosophy is the product of Greek thought. Pascal's statement recognized the prospect of a distinctly Jewish worldview that stood opposite to the Greek tradition.

Jewish Thinking as a Type of Thinking

The great Jewish theologian of the 20th century, Abraham Joshua Heschel, suggested that different types of thinking exist. Moreover, a particular thinking can be characterized as Jewish. The basis of his argument quickly on the nature of philosophy. Jenny Teichmann and Katherine C. Evans explain that,

---

God.' (Genesis 18:22). Abraham endures for ever. We are Abraham, Isaac, Jacob." Abraham Joshua Heschel, *God in Search of Man: A Philosophy of Judaism* (New York: JPS, 1955), 201.

"Philosophy is a study of problems which are ultimate, abstract, and very general. These problems are concerned with the nature of existence, knowledge, morality, reason, and human purpose."[2]

That being said, philosophy requires certain presuppositions, modes of thought, and types of evaluation. It, therefore, involves a particular kind of thinking.[3]

A good example is Aristotelian philosophy. Aristotle was the student of Plato, who, in turn, was the student of Socrates. Aristotle's logical discussions were conceived to provide a reasoning method through which a person could learn anything and everything.

For example, the Categories provides a system for describing things in terms of their properties, condition, and behavior. The elementary school student is often

---

[2] "Philosophy is a study of problems which are ultimate, abstract and very general. These problems are concerned with the nature of existence, knowledge, morality, reason and human purpose." Jenny Teichmann and Katherine C. Evans, *Philosophy: A Beginner's Guide* (Blackwell Publishing, 1999), 1.

[3] Abraham Joshua Heschel, *God in Search of Man: A Philosophy of Judaism* (New York: JPS, 1955), 14.

introduced to the concept of the genus, species, and family in biology. Still, Aristotle believed this system could be applied to all areas of human knowledge. In his *On Interpretation, Prior Analytics and Posterior Analytics,* Aristotle introduced the nature of deductive inference, i.e., logical conclusion, outlining his categorical reasoning system from true propositions.

The Greek tradition on science and government has been profound in Western civilization and indeed the world. Let me note that I do not believe anything is inherently wrong with the Greek tradition related to the sciences and government. However, in the context of religious faith, our concern is not the physical sciences but the realm of the spirit. As Heschel notes,

> "The truth is that revelation is a problem that eludes scientific inquiry;"[4]

---

[4] Abraham Joshua Heschel, *God in Search of Man: A Philosophy of Judaism* (New York: JPS, 1955), 220.

The classical Greek writers were not concerned with the sublime. The sublime is arguably Jewish by birth.[5]

The impact of Greek thought on the Jewish world was inescapable, just as the non-Jewish world has always impacted the Jewish community. Many Jews embraced Hellenism and saw no contradiction or problem in melding "Jerusalem and Athens." Heschel characterized the Hellenization of Jewish theology as an attempt to equate Plato and Moses. Those who embraced this view believed that they said the same thing. Only Plato would say it in Greek and Moses in Hebrew. Consequently, this approach saw Moses as a sort of Hebrew Plato.

Despite the attempts of Philo of Alexandria, Rabbi Moses ben Maimon, and many others to understand Jewish thinking and Greek thinking as expressing the same ideas and truth, the dissimilarities between the two exist at even linguistic levels. The more significant distinction

---

[5] Ibid., 37.

between the two types of thinking in a variety of areas become apparent.[6]

Hans-Georg Gadamer noted a critical difference between Jewish and Greek thought. He wrote that " Greek philosophy more or less begins with the insight that a *word is only a name*, i.e., that it does not represent true being." That fact provided Plato, for example, with the basis of his ontological views. For Plato, language was inherently imperfect and conditional; perfection is only possible in the domain of unchanging forms.

A typical example given to explain Plato's philosophy is to speak of the *real* and the *ideal*. A physical object, for instance, a chair, exists. Still, there is an ideal version of this object free from the chair's defects and imperfections in our physical reality. The Greek bias towards the supposed insufficiency of language created a quest for a purely rational system of symbols. Ideas in the Greek mind are perfect. For the Greeks, especially Plato, the ultimate

---

[6] Epistemology refers to the theory of knowledge. In particular to its methods, validity, and range. Ontology is the philosophical study of the nature of being, existence, and reality.

world is a world of ideal forms. The ultimate realities are *ideas*.

In contrast, the Hebrew understanding of a word (i.e., *davar)* denotes a name and a thing. The Hebrew word conveys the meaning as well as a description of the object or being in question.[7] Thorleif Boman argued that another fundamental difference between Hebrew and Greek exists. In Hebrew, Boman contends, verbs reflect motion, dynamic variety; in contrast, Greek verbs are static or harmonic. For Boman, this grammatical note highlights the differences between Hebrew and Greek thought as innate.[8] Hebrew and Greek thought are inherently different.

For the Hebrew Bible, the ultimate reality is God. For Greek thought, the goal is to define universal categories.

---

[7] Susan A. Handelman, *The Slayer of Moses: The Emergence of Rabbinic Interpretation in Modern Literary Theory* (Albany: State University of New York Press), 3-5. I. Rabbinowitz also notes that the word *davar meaning* both thing and word, nevertheless implies something different that the Greek concept of thing. It implies reality or as Rabbinowitz states "the word is the reality in its most concentrated, compacted, essential form" and is an aspect of the divine creative force." Ibid., 32.

[8] Thorleif Boman *Hebrew Thought Compared with Greek* (New York: W.W. Norton & Company, 1960), 27-28.

In Hebrew, the emphasis is on the unique and the individual. For Aristotle, language is conventional. Hence, Aristotle's law of exclusion tells us that we can have either "P or not P." However, in Jewish thought, "P and not P" can exist simultaneously.

The numerous conflicts which are found in the Talmud reflect the idea that "these and these are both words of the Living God."[9] Aristotle considers only one dimension of meaning in the text instead of the rabbinic view that there are 70 faces (i.e., multiple dimensions) to the Torah's meaning. The Pirkei Avot, the Sayings of the Fathers, tells us regarding the Torah,

> "Ben Bag Bag says: 'Turn it and turn it since everything is in it. And in it should you look, and grow old and be worn in it, and from it do not move since there is no characteristic greater than it.' "[10]

---

[9] Eruvin 13b.
[10] Pirkei Avot 5:22.

CHAPTER 2

Jewish Thinking and Hellenistic Thought

If the Hellenistic world can be seen as the critical intellectual prism of Western thought, then the Bible and the classical Jewish tradition found in the Talmud (i.e., the Mishnah and the Gemara) must be viewed as the foundational sources of Jewish thinking. We have already encountered some differences between Jewish and Greek thought. What are other differences between Jewish thinking and Greek thinking, and do any similarities or intersections exist?.

For the authors of the Biblical texts and the framers of the earliest written body of Jewish Oral Law, the Mishnah, the goal of their inquiries was the revelation of God's fundamental character in His Creation and the connectedness of all things. God was neither the subject of *classification* nor the object of *generalization*. The primary concern of science and western philosophical inquiry regarding, for example, the existence of the world was the matter of causality – the relationship between the cause and effect and the components involved in the process.[1]

However, the Bible, as Heschel notes, envisions the creation of the world as the interaction and relationship between the Creator of the universe and His Creation, though the two are two incomparable entities.[2] Heschel relates the following:

> "Judaism a religion of history, a religion of time. The God of Israel was not found primarily in the facts of nature. He spoke through events in history. While other deities of other peoples were associated with places or things, the God of the prophets was the God of events: the Redeemer from slavery, the

---

[1] Abraham Joshua Heschel, *God in Search of Man: A Philosophy of Judaism* (New York: JPS, 1955), 16
[2] Ibid., 16.

Revealer of the Torah, manifesting Himself in events of history rather than in things or places."[3]

The God of the universe breaks through another dimension to create the world and, most importantly, from the perspective of the Bible, to engage with His most precious creation, man. For the Greek philosophers, causality is of primary importance; for the Biblical authors, the very *source* of the causality overrides any other concern. For example, Aristotelian philosophy is characterized by its desire for order through the classification of all created things. The Bible presents Creation as the act of God.[4]

The ideal individual of the Hebrew Bible is the person of *faith*. For Greek thought, the perfect person is the *rational* individual. In contrast to the rational individual, the person of faith, as reflected in the Hebrew Bible, is not concentrated on universal forms, the abstract, or the theoretical, but is wholly connected to those things that are particular, specific, and concrete. The Biblical man

---

[3] Ibid., 200. The emphasis placed on Shabbat is an excellent example.
[4] Ibid., 16.

embraces all of life and experiences as a whole person with emotions, passion, feeling, and struggle. Perhaps the best example is that of King David. He embraced God in battle, in song, in love, and in distress.

In contrast, the Greek ideal for man was the detachment of man's reason from his animalistic needs and emotions.[5] Logic is the sole vehicle through which all things should be viewed, especially the Divine. For the Bible, man is to love and know God, with all his heart, soul, and strength, and this is manifest in his obedience to God's divine law, the Torah. This is the core of the most critical statement or prayer in Judaism, the *Shema*.[6]

As found in the Hebrew Bible and Aristotelian philosophy, the differences do not end here. A primary concern of Aristotelian philosophy is the matter of ontology or the essence of being. The essence of being, however, is not a

---

[5] William Barret, *Irrational Man: A Study in Existential Philosophy* (New York: Double Day, 1958), 68-69.

[6] Deuteronomy 6:4–9.

concern of the Bible. The relationship between Creation and the revelation of the Creator and His will is.[7]

The Bible avoids the world's programmatic definition as the mathematical sciences do by appealing to the unique and unprecedented. Philosophy concerns itself with the analysis, investigation, explanation, and generalization of the universe. In the case of Aristotle, the emphasis lies not in the value of the particular, but rather in the genus or class it belongs to so much so that Israel I. Efros states: "Thus the Greeks cared for the group and abandoned the individual, but it is not so with the Hebraic spirit."[8] The concern of Jewish thinking is the purification and sanctification of the person and Creation.[9]

---

[7] Abraham Joshua Heschel, *God in Search of Man: A Philosophy of Judaism* (New York: JPS, 1955), 16.

[8] Israel I. Efros, *Ancient Jewish Philosophy* (Detroit: Wayne University, 1964), 151.

[9] Abraham Joshua Heschel, *God in Search of Man: A Philosophy of Judaism* (New York: JPS, 1955), 16.

Greek and Hebraic Sources of Knowledge

In the Greek philosophical dialects, the philosopher always searches for truth and begins his quest by asking what the definition of truth is. These dialects always start with the "what" question. *What is the essence of truth?*

The philosopher begins by asking for a definition. An example of this is found in Socrates' famous inquiry as to what is a human being. A student responds that man is an animal. However, what kind, Socrates asks. A student answers that man is a biped. In response, Socrates brings a chicken to his lecture and asserts that a chicken must be a man according to the definition offered. A student clarifies that man is a featherless biped. Socrates returns the next day with a featherless chicken and so forth until the *definition* is refined.

Greek thought always attempts to define and classify. The Greeks were forever focused on theoretical knowledge's perfection, as reflected in its inherently creedal nature. The Bible, however, is not concerned with universal concepts or with definitions. The Biblical mind is interested in the description of complementary opposites.

Even Jacob Neusner, who asserts a measure of commonality of methodology in Aristotelian philosophy and the inductive methodology of the Mishnah, recognizes the critical differences between the God of Aristotle and his way of thinking and the God of Abraham and Jewish thought.[10] A review of the taxonomic method of Aristotle, Jacob Neusner suggests, permits a comparison between the philosophical approach of Greco-Roman thinking and the methodological framework of the Mishnah.

Such a comparison begins by using the standard classification method (i.e., genus and species and a fundamental pillar of Aristotelian philosophy). However, this approach already assumes that things or, for that matter, people are subject to classification. Classification

---

[10] Jacob Neusner, *Judaism as Philosophy, The Method and Message of the Mishnah* (Baltimore: The Johns Hopkins University Press, 1991), 244, 250.

implies that things have traits that are essential and indicative but also maintain similarities with other things.[11]

According to Neusner, therein lies the direct contact and intersection between Judaism's philosophy of hierarchical classification and Aristotle's philosophical methods. However, the similarity ends there, for the philosophers' goals and the rabbis of the Mishnah are strikingly different.[12] While commonality can be found in the desire to impart coherence to knowledge and experience, Aristotle's goal resides in *discovering the final causes of all things, their purpose, and the origin of their movement and change.* Aristotle viewed philosophical inquiry as producing a body of judgments which defined the connections between things and properties in the world. For Aristotle, the investigation into the immobile mover explains the eternity of the cosmic processes. The primary mover is necessary to explain

---

[11] Jacob Neusner argues that the priestly authorship of Genesis 1:1-2:4 with its creation of order out of chaos itself provides an understanding and use a hierarchical classification of all things. Jacob Neusner, *Judaism as Philosophy, The Method and Message of the Mishnah* (Baltimore: The Johns Hopkins University Press, 1991), 245.

[12] Jacob Neusner, *Judaism as Philosophy, The Method and Message of the Mishnah* (Baltimore: The Johns Hopkins University Press, 1991), 253.

the source of the motion of all things. The first cause, as the origin of all things, interestingly enough, is not the primary concern.[13]

Syllogistic Thinking versus Juxtaposition

Aristotle's contribution to a new type of thinking was his Creation of syllogistic logic. Its dependence on a subject-predicate relationship marks syllogistic reasoning (i.e., If A and B, then C) between two statements. Subsequently, this method became the form of all judgments and reasoning. Perhaps the most famous of these is the following:

All men are mortal;

Socrates is a man;

Therefore Socrates is mortal.

For Aristotle, this is the ideal model of thinking since it indicates the definition or classification of the subject (object in question) and ties this to the predicate providing its

---

[13] Ibid., 254.

description. As Aristotle notes, "It is necessary that every demonstration and every syllogism should prove either that something belongs or that it does not, and this either universally or in part." [14]

In contrast, the Sages of Israel embraced a type of thinking entirely different from syllogistic reasoning, which was based on another basis of relational inference. Rabbinic thought calls for a multi-faceted focus on words and their relationships to include the physical characteristics and shapes of letters and their location in a sacred text.[15]

The Rabbis also frequently employed the juxtaposition of topics as a tool in their logical inquiry. Juxtaposition refers to the nearness of ideas concerning each other. In this context, it relates to the *physical placement* of biblical verses with other verses. The use of juxtaposition to reach logical inference between seemingly unrelated passages

---

[14] An. Pr. 1.23-40b23.
[15] Susan A. Handelman, *The Slayer of Moses: The Emergence of Rabbinic Interpretation in Modern Literary Theory* (Albany: State University of New York Press), 17.

reflects the rabbis' adoption of a thinking relational in nature as opposed to the ontological basis of syllogistic thinking.

One clear example of juxtaposition to reach a practical decision is the rabbinic determination of meaning and categories of work. The passage in Ten Commandments forbidding work on the Sabbath does not define work.[16] Is it physical labor or merely labor required to earn a living? The Torah does not specify, and it is not until the book of Nehemiah that we find a reference to additional specific prohibitions. However, the description of the labor necessary to construct the *Mishkan* (i.e., the Tabernacle) in Exodus 25:8-31:2, and its juxtaposition with Exodus 31:13-17 does provide 39 categories of labor and hence the rabbinic conclusion that these are the 39 types of work forbidden on the Sabbath.[17]

---

[16] Exodus 20:10.
[17] Ibid. 24. The coherence of rabbinic thought lies it its intrinsic relationship between ideas characterized by a distinct though flexible body. Max Kadushin, *Organic Thinking: A Study in Rabbinic Thought* (JTS: New York, 1938), 6.

CHAPTER 3

Polarity in Jewish Thought

Western philosophy heavily emphasized systematic approaches to speculative theology. As noted, Western philosophical tradition is heavily reliant on Aristotelian logic, which considers logical consistency as the ultimate factor in deciding the legitimacy of a system of thought.[1]

While many Jewish thinkers have sought to impose a systematic approach to Jewish thought, neither biblical nor rabbinic sources consider theological concepts' systematization as fundamental. Systematic thinking in the Aristotelian vein is foreign to Judaism. In contrast, Jewish thought approaches theology and the nature of God's

---

[1] Byron L. Sherwin, *Towards a Jewish Theology* (Lewiston: Edwin Mellen Press: 1991), 17.

interaction with man via revelation through recognition of polarities.[2]

Abraham Joshua Heschel proposed that Jewish thought and life can only be understood in terms of the tension between conflicting ideas.[3] Hence Jewish religious thought articulates its worldview in terms of complementary opposites characterized by tension and contradiction. Heschel was once asked to explain *the* Jewish view on a particular subject. He responded that there were many Jewish views and each had its tributaries and streams.[4]

Polarity as the Pillar of Jewish Theology

Judaism recognizes the existence of polarities on two different levels. It recognizes them in the manner in which God reveals Himself to and interacts with His Creation. For example, Judaism recognizes the polarities in the

---

[2] Ibid., 17.

[3] Abraham Joshua Heschel, *God in Search of Man* (New York: Farras, Straus, Giroux, 1955), 341.

[4] Sherwin, Byron L., PhD. "What is Jewish Thinking?" Lecture, Spertus Institute of Jewish Learning and Leadership, Chicago, 2006.

existence of obedience (mitzvah) and sin, of love and fear, collective responsibility, and individuality, to name a few.[5]

It also recognizes God's interaction with the world as characterized by justice and mercy, divine intervention, and concealment, and as Abraham Joshua Heschel notes, God's promise of heavenly reward for obedience and the requirement to serve God for His own sake.[6]

Judaism embraces the existence of polarity as the very basis of its theological system. Aggadah and Halakhah are the two pillars of Jewish theology. Halakhah is derived from the word *halakh* (i.e., to walk). Halakhah provides regularity, structure, and direction on the performance of a divine or mundane act. It provides structure, definitions, boundaries, and law- how to walk in a fixed path. The word Aggadah refers to the telling or recounting of something. Aggadah is the vehicle which the rabbis used to express the complexity of their relationship and search for God and their interaction with man. Whereas Halakhah

---

[5] Abraham Joshua Heschel, *God in Search of Man* (New York: Farras, Straus, Giroux, 1955), 341.
[6] Ibid., 341.

deals with specificity, Aggadah serves to communicate the broader picture of life and those areas that are undefinable in terms of Halakhah. Halakhah tells us how; Aggadah tells us why. The existence of one without the other is unimaginable.[7]

Polarity in Biblical Literature

The struggle to understand God's presence serves as an example of such tension and polarity in Jewish thought. Distraught with suffering and surrounded by antagonists, Job comments on the mysterious nature of God and the inability of a man to "know" or find God:

> "But if I go East- He is not there; West – I still do not perceive Him; North –since He is concealed, I do not behold Him; South – He is hidden, and I cannot see Him."[8]

King David nevertheless describes the presence of God as ubiquitous, noting:

---

[7] Ibid., 336-337.
[8] Job 23: 8-9.

"Whither shall I go from Thy Spirit? Or whither shall I flee from Thy presence? If I ascend to heaven, Thou art there; If I make my bed in *Sheol*, behold Thou art there." [9]

God, it appears, then is both immanent and transcendent. The prayer book provides a further description of this in its description of God in the heavenly realm. The word *Kadosh* or holiness is used about the uniqueness of God's existence and character. The *Kedushah* of the *Amidah* and the *Et Shem* preceding the *Ahava Rabah* express the same position:

"Holy, Holy, Holy is the LORD, Master of Legions."

The angelic beings who dwell in the spiritual world, and stand at the summit of the universe themselves, proclaim that God is unique, separate, and even distant from them. The distance and separation between man and God seems immeasurable. David confidently states that the LORD is near to all who call Him, to all who call Him with

---

[9] Psalm 139:7-8.

sincerity.[10] For David, God is transcendent, but also hears the prayers of His Creation.

The Greeks viewed the universe as the total sum of all that existed. The gods were even part of it. In Plato's dialogue titled Timaeus, he states, "The world (cosmos) the same for all, was not made by any god or man but was always, and is, and shall be."[11]

The Bible, in contrast, describes the world as an act of Creation, of the one true Creator. The prophet Isaiah relates, "The heaven is My throne, and the earth is My footstool." [12]

The Problem of Evil

The dilemma of evil also serves as an example of complementary opposites in Jewish thought. Rabbi Byron

---

[10] Psalm 145:18; "Holy, Holy, Holy is the L-rd, Master of Legions, the whole world is full of his glory." Isaiah 6:3.

[11] Cited in Abraham Joshua Heschel, *God in Search of Man* (New York: Farras, Straus, Giroux, 1955), 91.

[12] Isaiah 66:1. Isaiah 40:17 also states: "All the nations are as nothing before Him' they are accounted by Him as things of nought, and vanity."

Sherwin, in discussing the dilemma of theodicy, contended that monotheistic faith must ultimately recognize God as the source of all things, including evil. Evil must be understood as being created by God as the book of Lamentations notes: "Is it not from the mouth of the Most High that good and evil come? [13]

The prophet Isaiah even states, "I form light and darkness I *make good and evil-* I the LORD do all these things."[14]

Without this polarity and the existence of evil, Rabbi Sherwin argues, good would be unrecognizable and unattainable. Consequently, the free moral choice between good and evil would become meaningless. Accordingly, the *Sefer Yetzirah* states:

> "God has set each thing to correspond with another; the good against the evil, and the evil against the good; good from good and evil from good; the good marks out the evil and the evils marks out the good;

---

[13] Lamentations 3:38.
[14] Isaiah 45:7; See also Job 2:20 and Ecclesiastes 7:14.

good is reserved for the good ones and evil is reserved for the evil ones..." [15]

Such a view ultimately serves to position God as the source of all things. The *Midrash Terumah* states: "God created everything in pairs, one set against the other," and Rabbi Judah Loew of Prague asserted that all things are created out of one essence or its opposite. Biblical theology holds that a single God must embrace a polarity of evil and good even as Rabbi Sherwin noted: "of the benevolent and the demonic, of the merciful and the sinister." [16]

The Nature of Man

The existence of the evil inclination underscores the struggle man faces and the seeming impossibility of his excess over the evil. Man is viewed as both wholly corrupt and yet capable of righteousness. Psalms 14:1 reveals:

"The LORD looked down from heaven upon the children of men, to see if there were any that did

---

[15] Sefer Yetsirah 6:2.
[16] Byron L. Sherwin, *Towards a Jewish Theology* (Lewiston: Edwin Mellen Press: 1991), 70.

understand and seek God. They are all gone aside, they are all together become filthy: there is none that doeth good, no, not one."

The Hebrew Scriptures also provide a very different view of man and his ability to achieve righteousness, as Psalm 146:8 states:

"The LORD sets prisoners free; The LORD restores sight to the blind; The LORD makes those who are bent stand straight; the LORD loves the righteous."

The nature of man serves as an example of polarities in Jewish thought. In Psalm 90, ascribed to Moses, the Psalmist acknowledges the fate of man: "You (God) return man to dust; you decreed, 'Return you, mortals.' " In the same breath, the Psalmist declares that though man is made of dust, the LORD, Himself, is man's refuge in every generation. Genesis 1: 27 also notes, "And God created man in His image, in the image of God He created him; male and female He created them."

Polarity as Essential to All Things

Polarity then provides Jewish thought with balance. Polarity, as Abraham Joshua Heschel explains, is essential to all things. The Zohar describes the world we live in as the world of separation because our world is characterized by tension, ambiguity, and discrepancies. That tension is found in all aspects of life, including a Torah life, yet all tensions end in God in whom there are no dichotomies.[17]

Greek thought is characterized by dispassion and apathy. Reflection rather than attachment and involvement is characteristic of Greek thought. For the Greeks, beauty and health are viewed as a balance. Lack of health is an imbalance. Balance is beautiful. Beauty is a form of good. No aesthetic thing is bad.

In Judaism, however, there is a separation: Good can exist without the moral. A person can be ugly but could be moral. Greek thought does not seem to agree. Ethics

---

[17] Abraham Joshua Heschel, *God in Search of Man* (New York: Farras, Straus, Giroux, 1955), 347.

are not differentiated in rabbinic thought from manners.

In Western thought, there is no connection.

CHAPTER 4

The Rabbinic Mind

In rabbinic thought, values are expressed in specific terms, with every value having their own designation or name. These values consist of ideas that function in everyday life. Because they reflect the continually changing nature and circumstance of daily existence, they, in turn, are themselves malleable. Defining these concepts as definitive statements is, therefore, untenable. They are, as Max Kadushin argues, undefined concepts. Yet, this lack of concretization allows for rabbinic thought to be highly flexible and responsive to the human experience's differentiated nature.[1]

Any rabbinic concept or idea may unite with another rabbinic concept.[2] Rabbinic ideas or value concepts, as Max Kadushin labels them, are inseparable from normal, day to day experiences and reflect a particular natural character.[3] This very "naturalness" and character of so many rabbinic statements that reflect an everyday quality have led many to question the existence of an organizing principle in rabbinic thought.[4]

"It is precisely the naturalness, the everyday quality of the rabbinic Midrashim that led the modern

---

[1] Max Kadushin, *The Rabbinic Mind* (New York: Jewish Theological Seminary, 1952), 1-2. Kadushin further states: "A well-ordered, logical, hence uniform, system negates that very complexity which is the chief characteristic of human motives and conduct." Max Kadushin, *Organic Thinking: A Study in Rabbinic Thought* (New York: Bloch Publishing, 1938), v.

[2] Ibid., 31.

[3] Ibid., 31.

[4] Max Kadushin, *The Rabbinic Mind* (New York: Jewish Theological Seminary, 1952), 31. the person of faith as reflected in the Bible is neither concentrated on universal forms, the abstract, nor, theoretical but is wholly connected to those things that are particular, specific, and concrete. The Biblical man embraces all of life and its experiences as a whole person with emotions, passion, feeling, and struggle.

authorities…accustomed to philosophic and ethical systems in which deliberate, careful, effortful demonstration is the rule to despair of finding any principle of organization in rabbinic thought. They looked, apparently, for an organizing principle which would systematize the many and varied rabbinic statements, and *they soon found that these statements would not fit into any logical scheme.*" [5]

However, the coherence found in rabbinic thought is one that exists in the natural relationship between concepts. Max Kadushin argues that in rabbinic thought, logic can be understood in the following manner.

"All the concepts employed bear an organic relationship to one another, interweaving with each other so as to produce a definite, though an extremely flexible, pattern."[6]

---

[5] Max Kadushin, *The Rabbinic Mind* (New York: Jewish Theological Seminary, 1952), 31.

[6] Max Kadushin, *Organic Thinking: A Study in Rabbinic Thought* (New York: Bloch Publishing, 1938), 7. The flexibility of rabbinic thought is perhaps shown in the range of its antecedent, biblical thought. In contrast to the nature of Western philosophy which heavily emphasizes a definition and categorical approach to knowledge and all things, Jewish thinking approaches the nature of God's interaction with man through

Rabbinic concepts do not provide a logical or systematic character found in creedal models of faith or philosophy. Neither do they reflect a system in which a specific hierarchical order exists. Instead, rabbinic thought is characterized by a non-hierarchical pattern like coherence among its various concepts.[7] Kadushin states that because of this, a certain indeterminacy exists.

> "The coherence of organic thinking renders the 'zone of insecurity' or indeterminacy a characteristic alike of rabbinic theology and of social values in general. Since no rabbinic concept inevitably follows from any other concept, any given situation is not necessarily interpreted by a single combination of concepts."[8]

For Kadushin, while many ideas exist in rabbinic thought, four fundamental concepts are vital. The four concepts are

---

recognition of polarities. Byron L. Sherwin, *Towards a Jewish Theology* (Lewiston: Edwin Mellen Press: 1991), 17. "Neither biblical nor rabbinic literature, for example considered the systematization of ideas either necessary or desirable."

[7] Max Kadushin, *A Conceptual Approach to the Mekilta* (New York: Jewish Theological Seminary, 1969), 2.

[8] Max Kadushin, *Organic Thinking: A Study in Rabbinic Thought* (New York: Bloch Publishing, 1938), 13.

as follows: God's loving-kindness, His justice, Torah, and Israel. Kadushin is quick to reemphasize that while these concepts are fundamental to understanding rabbinic thought, they are not "like the articles of a creed," which reflect positions of varying importance. They are all of equal importance.[9]

According to Kadushin, all rabbinic concepts are composed of the four fundamental ideas. Kadushin provides several examples to illustrate the interrelationship of these concepts. The idea of sanctifying the Name of God or *Kiddush Hashem* is ultimately brought about when the God of Israel is recognized as the One True God. It is also brought about when the children of Israel demonstrate a willingness to die as martyrs when necessary. It is also achieved when the Torah's standard and God's justice and love reflected in the Torah are established.[10]

Kadushin provides another example to illustrate the fundamental relationship between these concepts. The idea of *Malchut Shamayim,* recognizing and accepting God's sovereignty, is demonstrated when the children of Israel accept

---

[9] Ibid., 6.
[10] Ibid., 7.

this by declaration, as in the case of Mount Sinai. It is also reflected in the study and observance of the Torah. Finally, it is demonstrated in recognition of His love and justice.[11]

Aggadic statements reflect the organismic nature of rabbinic concepts and, in fact, often reflect several ideas. Hence rabbinic ideas are potentially concurrent with each other. Nevertheless, despite the number of ideas present, a single idea or expression can be derived from a particular statement because the concepts in question are interwoven.[12] This feature of rabbinic thought allows for flexibility, depending on the circumstance. Hence rabbinic thought allows for concentration on one idea and another as "needed." Religious beliefs can, therefore, be communicated without creating or referencing them as creedal principles.[13]

On a practical level, these "impulses," as Solomon Schecter noted, produced a vast range of articulation. So in one instance, emphasis might be placed on God's mercy when the community faced persecution and needed solace.

---

[11] Ibid., 7.

[12] Max Kadushin, *A Conceptual Approach to the Mekilta* (New York: Jewish Theological Seminary, 1969), 18-19.

[13] Max Kadushin, *The Rabbinic Mind* (New York: Jewish Theological Seminary, 1952), 14.

It might also produce a focus on Divine punishment if the community's observance of the Torah was waning.[14]

Logical Thinking in Rabbinic Thought

The lack of definition and systemization in rabbinic thought does not imply that rational thinking is not present or necessary. As Kadushin notes, no individual can live without a degree or logical or inferential thinking.[15] The rabbis use consistent methodologies for interpreting biblical texts, as evidenced by the *Seven Rules of Hillel*, the *Thirteen Middot of Rabbi Ishmael*, and the *Thirty Two Middot of Eliezer be Yose ha-Gelili*.[16] The rabbis scrutinized and compared texts reviewed the linguistic possibilities of words, and utilized the aforementioned hermeneutic rules.[17] Kadushin notes the following:

---

[14] Solomon Schechter, *Aspects of Rabbinic Theology: Major Concepts of the Talmud* (New York: Schocken Books, 1961), 12.

[15] Max Kadushin, *Organic Thinking: A Study in Rabbinic Thought* (New York: Bloch Publishing, 1938), 202.

[16] H.L. Strack and Gunter Stemberger, *Introduction to the Talmud and Midrash* (Minneapolis: Fortress Press, 1996), 16-30.

[17] Max Kadushin, *Organic Thinking: A Study in Rabbinic Thought* (New York: Bloch Publishing, 1938), 219.

> "…the Rabbis use logical procedures in order to interpret biblical texts and also in their search for ways to extend and deepen the concretizations of the concepts…the rabbinic method of interpretation subjects the biblical texts to minute analysis."[18]

The statements made by the rabbis must be viewed against the backdrop of organic thought. This fact leads to a greater understanding of rabbinic thought's nature and the reasonable nature of otherwise convoluted statements outside of the natural reflection process.[19] Furthermore, the use of "logical" methodologies in interpreting biblical texts did not lead to consistent interpretation. Any verse could be construed in various ways. The well-known verse in Psalm 133:1, "How good and pleasant it is where brothers live in unity," could be understood to refer to Aaron's relationship with God as well as relating to the various stages in a person's life and how they stand in harmony with the study of the Torah.[20] Most significant is the differentiation in the use

---

[18] Ibid., 203-204.
[19] Ibid., 203.
[20] Ibid., 205.

of logical methods between rabbinic thought and creedal-philosophical thinking. Kadushin states:

> "In no case do they [i.e., the Rabbis] take to demonstrate logically the existence of the concepts themselves."[21]

Since most aggadic statements are homilies on biblical passages, the relationship and approach to rabbinic thought are necessary. The logical approach to studying and interpreting biblical texts has already been made. Our concern here is the relationship of rabbinic concepts to the Bible.

While rabbinic value concepts are not directly lifted from the biblical texts, they are not foreign to biblical ideas. As Kadushin states, all rabbinic concepts are rooted in the Bible.[22] Furthermore, an intimate relationship exists between rabbinic thought and the Bible.[23] At the minimum, the Bible presents antecedents of the concepts found in rabbinic thought. In other cases, such as the fundamental rabbinic concepts of God's love and justice, the Torah, and Israel, the

---

[21] Ibid., 206.

[22] Max Kadushin, *A Conceptual Approach to the Mekilta* (New York: Jewish Theological Seminary, 1969), 6.

[23] Max Kadushin, *Organic Thinking: A Study in Rabbinic Thought* (New York: Bloch Publishing, 1938), 219.

Bible contains views very much reflective of the former.[24] The similarities do not obscure that in many instances, words with dual usage (i.e., Biblical and Rabbinic) do have different meanings. Kadushin notes:

> "In the Bible, Israel is always a collective noun referring to the people as a collective entity, and this meaning is retained in rabbinic literature…As used by the Rabbis, however, the word may also designate the members of the people individually as well, and then the parts of speech used in connection with the noun are in the singular, and "Israel" means an Israelite."[25]

Even in cases where rabbinic concepts do not appear in name in biblical texts, such as *Malchut Shamayim, Olam Haba,* and *Talmid Chacham,* among others, the biblical text maintains the antecedents or fundamentals are found there. As Kadushin states:

> "The idea of God's justice, for example, is represented in rabbinic literature by a conceptual term,

---

[24] Ibid., 219.
[25] Max Kadushin, *A Conceptual Approach to the Mekilta* (New York: Jewish Theological Seminary, 1969), 9.

Middat ha-Din, a purely rabbinic term. But the idea itself, it is hardly necessary to say, is written large upon page after page in the Bible, even though it is not crystallized there in an analogous conceptual term." [26]

The Bible itself is the organic complex from which the rabbinic organic complex emerges.[27] As shown, Rabbinic value concepts do not follow neatly defined categories. Value concepts and hence, rabbinic thought are dynamic. They cannot be organized into a static system. Propositional statements do not define their meaning.[28]

---

[26] Ibid. 6.

[27] Max Kadushin, *Organic Thinking: A Study in Rabbinic Thought* (New York: Bloch Publishing, 1938), 229.

[28] Max Kadushin, *The Rabbinic Mind* (New York: Jewish Theological Seminary, 1952), 31.

Chapter 5

Thinking about Judaism in Non-Jewish Ways

For normative Judaism, the challenge of embracing Jerusalem or Athens (in a metaphorical sense) was a real issue of tremendous significance. While Hellenism is a historical phenomenon, it represents the ever-present struggle toward assimilation and possible abandonment of Judaism by Jews caught between two competing worlds. This was perhaps most strikingly and violently seen in the Maccabean struggle but was also experienced intellectually and theologically in subsequent generations.

To the informed reader, as was mentioned previously, a reasonable objection might be raised as to the Jewish incorporation of non-Jewish thinking by even one of its greatest sages. Despite the enormous accomplishments of the

Spanish Rabbi, Moses ben Maimon in Jewish law, the collection and classification of Jewish law in his *Mishneh Torah* reveals but a bit of Rabbi Maimon's review of Judaism through the heavily influenced scope of Aristotelian philosophy.

While his philosophical masterpiece, the *Guide for the Perplexed*, is founded upon Aristotelian principles, his authorship of the *Thirteen Principles* of the Jewish faith as a definitive summary of the essence of Judaism may ultimately reveal Rabbi Moses ben Maimon's thinking about Judaism in non-Jewish ways.

Rabbi Maimon's principles of faith include God's existence, unity, incorporeality, and eternity. These statements are creedal expressions of philosophical ideas more akin to Christian doctrinal positions rather than assertions about the nature of God's interaction and relationship with Creation and Israel specifically.

As Abraham Joshua Heschel notes, Rabbi Maimon's creed is based on the premise that *ultimate reality is realized in ideas*.[1] This is not to exclude the contributions of Rabbi Maimon to Jewish thought. Far from it. Rabbi Maimon, as a

---

[1] Ibid., 21.

physician, mathematician, dietician, Talmudist, and philosopher, remains in a class of his own and his insights are of critical importance in a subsequent chapter of this book. Our concern here, however, is his attempted synchronization between Jewish thought and the philosophical tradition.

Rabbi Maimon's creed then is based on the same philosophical approach as Aristotle. The Supreme Being's unchanging qualities, His immutable nature, and the articulation of God as ultimate perfection do not reflect the biblical and classical rabbinic view of describing God through His acts on behalf of Israel. The Exodus from Egypt, the splitting of the Sea of Reeds, and the revelation at Sinai are the events through which Judaism understands God.[2]

The generalizations of Aristotelian thought adopted by Rabbi Maimon regarding God's goodness or perfection or the essence of His being diverged from the Biblical picture of God's character revealed in specific instances for a particular people. The God of Israel is not known through the mere contemplation of the Divine nature but in

---

[2] Ibid., 20-21.

recognizing and awareness of His historic and ongoing acts of kindness.

Rabbi Maimon stands very far from the assertion made by Heschel regarding the nature of prophetic revelation. He is preoccupied with the ever-present challenge of the Bible's anthropomorphic description of God, His incorporeality, and a proper understanding of God's essence. Rabbi Maimon states:

> "It will be explained later that those who possess a *true knowledge* of God do not consider that He possesses many attributes but believe that these various attributes which describe His Might, Greatness, Power, Perfection, Goodness, etc. are identical, denoting *His Essence*, and not anything extraneous to *His Essence*."[3]

We need only to remember the classical creeds of early Christianity to find similarities between the importance of

---

[3] On the Homonyms in the Bible Chapter XX M. Friedlander, Moses Maimonides, *The Guide for the Perplexed* (New York: Dover Press, 1956), 29.

definition(s) that Greek thought placed and that Rabbi Maimon espoused. The Anathasian Creed reads:

> "Now this is the Catholic faith: We worship one God in the Trinity and the Trinity in unity, neither confusing the persons nor dividing the divine being. For the Father is one person, the Son is another, and the Spirit is still another. But the deity of the Father, Son, and Holy Spirit is one, equal in glory, coeternal in majesty. What the Father is, the Son is, and so is the Holy Spirit. Uncreated is the Father; uncreated is the Son; uncreated is the Spirit. The Father is infinite; the Son is infinite; the Holy Spirit is infinite. Eternal is the Father; eternal is the Son; eternal is the Spirit: And yet there are not three eternal beings, but one who is eternal; as there are not three uncreated and unlimited beings, but one who is uncreated and unlimited." [4]

Without any disrespect to Christians, I would suggest that this creed is a complicated exercise attempting to articulate

---

[4] The Athanasian Creed | Reformed Church in America, https://www.rca.org/resources/athanasian-creed (accessed January 03, 2017.

the Divine's ineffable nature, to define and reason through propositional statements, what the Bible instead seeks to *describe* the actions of the Creator. Once again, Rabbi Abraham Joshua Heschel explains:

> "The problem is no longer how to reconcile the Bible with Aristotle's view of the universe and of man, but rather: what is the Biblical view of the universe and of man's position in it? How should we understand ourselves in terms of Biblical thinking? The problem is: What are the ultimate questions of existence which religion comes to answer? What are the ideas a religious man stands for?" [5]

In Aristotelian thought, God is the perfect being. Thinking or contemplation is an ideal thing for a philosopher. Then God must spend all of his time thinking. What does He think about? He must reflect on perfect things. Since He is the only perfect thing, He must think about Himself, or else imperfect thoughts would enter His mind lowering Him. The two creeds, Maimonidean and Anathasian, lie in this domain and not in the world of traditional Jewish thinking.

---

[5] Abraham Joshua Heschel, *God in Search of Man: A Philosophy of Judaism* (New York: JPS, 1955), 22.

Christian doctrines, and in this case Maimonides, are attempting to answer Jewish issues in non-Jewish ways.

Perfection for the Greeks is to be static. For God to retain his perfection, he cannot change. He cannot have any relationships with imperfect beings. Perfection is to be intellectual. The Hebrew word for perfection is *shlemut- shalom,* meaning to be complete or whole. The God of the prophets is active. The Greek god is apathetic. The goal of human existence is to be indifferent, while the Hebrew notion is to be involved with the world and with the emotions. The gods of Greek tragedy, the gods, are ruled by necessity and moral volition and the rejection of faith. The Greeks regarded the elemental powers of Creation as holy. The referred to the holy rain and the holy light. The Bible, of course, warns against the religion of nature. The Scripture states:

> "Beware lest you lift up your eyes to heaven, and when you see the sun and the moon and the stars, all the host of heaven, you be drawn away and worship them." [6]

---

[6] Deuteronomy 4:19.

However, as Abraham Joshua Heschel asserts, the Hebrew prophets did not concern themselves with developing an idea of God or articulating a theory regarding God's essence. The prophets felt the presence of God as a tangible reality. As David notes in Psalm 145, "The LORD is close to all those who call upon Him." The prophets and the Psalmist alike *understood* God. They rejected the notion that a generalization or abstract theory of God was necessary to know God. While Maimonides seems preoccupied with the exposition of God's nature as the fundamental points of Judaism, the prophets were concentrated on describing and revealing God's act of Creation as responses to and concern for man. Heschel reminds of how Judaism understands God's compassion: "God's goodness is not a cosmic force but a specific act of compassion. We do not know it as it is, but as it happens." [7] Jewish existence is existence before a living and reachable God.

The Jewish philosophical tradition, as reflected in Maimonides, stresses the immateriality and unity of God. This allows for Michael Wyschogrod's explanation that the *via*

---

[7] Abraham Joshua Heschel, *God in Search of Man: A Philosophy of Judaism* (New York: JPS, 1955), 21.

negativa of Rabbi Maimon as the only possible approach of describing God. But this emphasis on a unity interpreted metaphysically removes the God of Abraham, Isaac, and Jacob from the realm of human understanding and produces nothing more than inconceivable; a God that, as Rabbi Byron Sherwin noted in a lecture, a person cannot pray to.

The prophets thought of God and man at the same time. Rabbi Maimon adopted the Hellenistic approach and saw a divide. The people cannot pray to a God that was described in abstract philosophical Aristotelian terms. Greco-Roman rational approaches are very different from Biblical-Rabbinic models. The God of the Bible is, for lack of a better term, a person. As Michael Wyschogrod notes, he appears as a character in its stories with expectations and is subject to emotions, which can grow disappointed, who becomes remorseful and, most importantly, faithful to those who trust in Him.[8]

This is arguably Rabbi Maimon's position, though his continued affirmation and dedication to the Torah separate

---

[8] Michael Wyschogrod, *The Body of Faith: God and the People of Israel* (Northvale: Aaronson, 1996), 84.

him from others acting independently of the Torah. The goal is a rational conclusion by deductive thought with an inescapable conclusion. Faith is relegated to an ascent of certain propositions.

For Hebrew thought, the goal is right doing. Hence, the moral virtues are most important, as evidenced through the observance of the Torah. Deductive and intuitive thinking is necessary, but this only leads to a partial knowledge or limited grasp of the truth. The Jewish faith is existentially based on a trust commitment and relationship. The central act in the Jewish faith is revelation, which is an act of relationship.

The well-read reader might offer Philo of Alexandria as proof that religious Jews also dabbled heavily in a world philosophy far before Rabbi Maimon and that Hellenization was not a Gentile Christian issue only in the early centuries of the Common Era. Indeed this was the case, and Jews have continued to not only dabble but seek to integrate Hellenistic thought within Judaism ever since the earliest cross-cultural encounters.

As we saw, Rabbi Maimon attempted to resolve and reconcile Jewish ideas and the world of Hellenistic thought.

While an admirable goal, he embraced a non-Jewish approach to Jewish thinking. More importantly, in Rabbi Moses ben Maimon's case, he remained firmly committed to the world of Judaism despite his complicated approach to and integration of Aristotelian philosophy in his spiritual quest. This is, of course, was not the path of emerging non-Jewish Christianity.

Rabbi Maimon's views were also contested within the Jewish community. The Maharal, Rabbi Judah Loew of Prague, while opposing philosophical inquiry, nevertheless embraced Kabbalistic thought, which itself was strongly influenced by Platonic ideas. Judah Loew of Prague argued that Kabbalah was an authentic way of Jewish thinking, and classical philosophy was not. To justify his acceptance of Kabbalah, Judah Loew of Prague pointed out that even the word Kabbalah comes from the root *kibel,* meaning tradition. That is, Kabbalah is the *mesorah* (i.e., authentic Jewish tradition). In contrast, "Jewish philosophy" is never referred to as the tradition or as *kibel.* For the Maharal, classical philosophy is instead the individual contemplation of the philosopher.

For the Maharal, philosophy is based on Greek thinking, which has several significant claims that are inherently inimical to Jewish life. The Maharal also pointed to the pseudo-work titled *Tefilato sh'Aristo -The Prayer of Aristotle* in which Aristotle repents and asks God for forgiveness for introducing ideas that were inimical to Judaism to buttress his attack on philosophical inquiry. For Judah Loew, authentic Jewish philosophy is Jewish thinking.

Rabbi Moses Isserles, however, argued against the Maharal's vehement opposition to all philosophical inquiry. Rabbi Isserles can be viewed as a reconciler between philosophical inquiry and mysticism. For Rabbi Isserles, there was no real clash between philosophy and mysticism. They are both a part of the tradition because they are the same thing. They speak about things in different ways, but both are legitimate ways of Jewish thinking.

For Rabbis Isserles, Plato, and the other Greek philosophers derived their knowledge from Jewish sources. He argued that the Jews invented philosophy and went as far as to assert that Plato was a disciple of King David and Solomon. His assertion led to consider how the Greeks espoused views that were inimical to Jewish thought and why philosophy had fallen out of favor in Jewish circles brought about because of the tribulations of Jewish life. According to Isserles, the Greeks learned philosophy but *corrupted* it by introducing various ideas that deviated from its Jewish foundations. As far as Isserles was concerned, the task of Jews was to reconstruct philosophy as it was initially conceived.

CHAPTER 6

Christianity and Greek Thinking

It may seem odd to include a chapter on Christianity in a book on Jewish thinking. However, Christianity is inextricably tied to the western Jewish experience. In the medieval period, the relationship was, unfortunately, often a negative one. The impact of Christian ideas or the rabbis' concern to respond to them was an ever-present need.

Today, especially in the United States, Christians and Jews enjoy a rapport unknown in previous centuries. While most Jews living in western countries do not fear Christian violence, the influence of Christianity on Judaism is strong and remains a concern. As Rabbi Byron Sherwin once noted. Jews in American think about Judaism in

Protestant terms. Because of this, I believe including a short chapter on Christianity is critical.

For the average individual, the differences between Judaism and Christianity can be summed up rather simply: Christians believe that Jesus is Israel's promised Messiah, the Son of God, or even God Himself made flesh, and Jews do not. Other than this, Jews and Christians share much in common and reflect the same fundamental faith. After all, they are monotheistic religions based on the Hebrew Bible's revelatory claims (i.e., the Old Testament in Christian circles) and teach an ethical, moral lifestyle. Other differences are merely attributable to cultural or linguistic issues.

However, things are not so simple, and while the messianic claims of Jesus are indeed an issue of significant dispute between Jews and Christians, I would venture to say that the critical demarcation between Judaism and Christianity is based more on the fundamental differences that reach the core of each religious tradition. The basis for this idea was a lecture given by Rabbi Byron Sherwin z"l.

In this sense, Jesus is not the dividing factor but rather one aspect of differentiation. Instead, the core issues are related to the fundamental differences between Jewish thinking and non-Jewish thinking, the answer to the question "who are the Jews?" and finally, Judaism's understanding of the Torah as the foundation of God's relationship with the Jewish people. These areas I contend are the real differences between these two historic monotheistic faiths, rather than the singular focus of who Jesus was or claimed to be.

As a brief note, I should add that the statements made regarding Christian perspectives throughout this chapter are not intended to minimize the complexity and diversity of thought existent in ancient and modern Christianity. They are instead designed to serve as the basis upon which Jewish reflections regarding the same issues can be addressed and understood. Moreover, the principal concern is to establish Jewish perspectives on the important topics of discussion.

The difference in thinking is our paramount concern because understanding and developing this idea is critical because how Jews and Christians approach the Bible, life, history, and theology are the by-product of the "philosophical" differences between them. All of the other points of disagreement are ultimately related to this matter. I hope to address them in a separate work.

My conclusion is that while Christianity was indeed founded upon Jewish ideas, its gradual expansion beyond the Jewish world transformed its worldview and thinking to that of religion understood and defined by distinctly Western and specifically Greco-Roman worldviews and philosophies. In the end, as Jacob Neusner asserts, the effect is that Judaism and Christianity say different things to different people in different ways.[1] For Christianity, the proper articulation of Orthodox faith through creedal expression is paramount.

As I noted, in Greek thought, the goal is *correct thinking*. Hence, we can understand Christianity's primary concern that the revelatory experience evidenced through the life and death of Jesus be adequately defined. The existence of

---

[1] Jacob Neusner, *Jews and Christians: The Myth of a Common Tradition* (Eugene: Wipf and Stock Publishers, 1991), 1.

dozens, if not hundreds of Christian denominations today, derived from doctrinal deviations and not primarily behavioral differences, prove this point. The focus is on "proper doctrine" or "belief," and these intellectual affirmations are superior to moral virtues. Anyone familiar with Protestant doctrinal statements realizes that the differences are often slight. A group separates from another because they see the former group as not embracing correct doctrine. Most of these variations are over seemingly theoretical views that have no immediate impact on the physical world.

A Christian might respond that while a difference between Jewish and non-Jewish thinking might indeed exist, Christian thought derived from the common base of the Hebrew Scriptures and informed by the pages of the New Testament- a product of Jews, should not stand in contrast to Jewish or Biblical thinking.

That argument bears weight to a certain extent. Christianity's incorporation and adoption of the western philosophical tradition as reflected in the great fathers of the early church (e.g., Justin, Origen, Augustine, etc.)

reveals the sieve through which the Hebrew Scripture as well as the New Testament writings were and are interpreted. Again Michael Wyschogrod notes:

> "There is no work of Jewish philosophy in existence, including Maimonides' Guide for the Perplexed, in which the duality of Judaism and philosophy is not clear and which is not therefore a work of dialogue in which Judaism and philosophy, each with its own identity and universe of discourse, talk to each other in full consciousness of their difference. This tension is not unique to Judaism; it can be found in many Christian authors. Augustine is a good example because he has his allegiance to Scripture and is also profoundly Platonic. Nevertheless, while it would be false to claim that a perfect fusion is achieved in Augustine, we come much closer to it than in any Jewish philosopher not only because Augustine lacks the inner distance that any Jew experiences toward Greek philosophy as a gentile enterprise but because he thinks of Christianity as

a set of beliefs that he is trying to define. Augustine...sees himself as the cutting edge of Christianity, engaged in a philosophic enterprise that is *at the very heart of this faith.*"[2]

Faith is, of course, critical to Judaism. With Ezra the Scribe's reforms as the starting point, Israelite religion was transformed from a religion solely expressed by its ethnic and geographically centered faith to a religious expression capable of existing far from the center of earlier Israelite cultic worship during the first Commonwealth.

Consequently, a metamorphosis from a people-nationhood self-understanding to that of a "confessional" community has been argued. This argument is linked to the loss of political independence and the redirected focus on the Temple's rebuilding as a cornerstone of Israelite/Jewish religious identity. The critical thing to remember is that Jewish identity was and is always tied to the covenant.

---

[2] Michael Wyschogrod, *The Body of Faith: God and the People of Israel* (Northvale: Aaronson, 1996), 72-73.

The Torah provides the Jewish community with a historical memory of a living God who selected the Jewish people from among the nations through whom He would be sanctified in history. Furthermore, according to Rabbi Hartman, the essential question in Judaism is not the nature of what is "good." This is already established as it states in the Tanakh, "It has been told you, O man, what is good and what the LORD does require of you."[3] The principal concern is the ability to embody the will of God in action. Therefore, God is revealed in the life history of the community " I am the LORD your God who brought (or because I brought) you out of the land of Egypt. As I previously noted, in Judaism, faith is memory.

Again, one need only to look at the premium placed on creedal formulations of belief in Christianity to understand the difference. The proper articulation of Christian faith is known by affirming a series of propositional statements. If a person deviates from these, they are rendered a heretic.

---

[3] Micah 6:8.

Christianity, in this sense, is concerned with the perfection of theoretical knowledge just as Plato was. At the extreme, the advent of the Protestant Reformation and its offspring in subsequent centuries reveals that even seemingly minor doctrinal deviations can spark the rise of a new denomination or create chasms in existing ones. The argument to borrow from Rabbi Maimon is the *true knowledge* of God, as reflected in a philosophical understanding. The mere fact that the contemporary Jewish experience manifests itself in three or four or five movements focusing principally on halakhic issues at most reveals the reality that Judaism understands its approach to knowing God" through a very different basis than its Christian counterpart.

Christians reading this book might raise a reasonable objection that the God of Israel is, in fact, the God of Jesus and hence also the God of Christianity. After all, doesn't the New Testament present Jesus and his followers as attending synagogue services, visiting the Temple in Jerusalem, and observing Jewish holidays? Many scholars have established the phenomena of early Jewish Christians and their continued attachment to Jewish life.

Nevertheless, it is clear that whatever the ongoing fidelity Jewish Christianity maintained towards a uniquely understood Jewish experience, emerging Gentile "Christianity" did not hold the same convictions and instead were much more open to ever-present Greco-Roman ideas. How can differences in "Thinking" between Jewish and Western philosophical notions about God be justly applied to Judaism and Christianity then?

The answer lies in the fact that despite their shared basis and connection to the Hebrew Bible (i.e., Old Testament), the world of Christianity is, in fact, the world of Greek and Roman experience. Though there is some evidence to suggest that perhaps one gospel or parts of it may have been written in Hebrew or Aramaic, the fact remains that the language in which the Gospels and the epistles of the New Testament were spread and eventually flourished in was Greek and ultimately Latin. The linguistic differences are essential in the primary sacred texts of Judaism and Christianity. Still, though communicated and initially written by religious Jews, the New Testament's language was interpreted through the prism of a very different cultural worldview and epistemological framework based on Greco-Roman thought by successive generations.

The greatest theologians of early Christianity, i.e., Justin, Tertullian, and Augustine, to name a few, were the products of contemporary philosophy that show the entry of a philosophical influence and worldview different from that of the Jewish people at critical junctures in Christian theological development. As Christianity distanced itself from its Jewish origins, it opened the door to Greco-Roman influences. This is perhaps understandable as Michael Wyschogrod notes:

> "The point then is that philosophic consciousness is present in the very origins of Christianity mainly because Christianity is born at a time when the philosophic consciousness is already developed. This is not true of Judaism. Judaism comes into a world in which the story still reigns

supreme…Judaism being much older, is born into a pre-philosophic world." [4]

There is much that Judaism and Christianity share in common. Jewish thinking ultimately divides them.

---

[4] Michael Wyschogrod, *The Body of Faith: God and the People of Israel* (Northvale: Aaronson, 1996), 55.

CHAPTER 7

Yehuda Halevi and Moses ben Maimon

While his works betray some Platonic influence, the overall views of Yehudah HaLevi do not belong to any particular philosophical school.[1] In his fact, HaLevi's major philosophical work, *The Book of Argument and Proof in Defense of the Despised Faith,* popularly known as the *Kuzari,* includes a severe critique of philosophical speculation. In contrast, Maimonides' works reflect a deep commitment to Aristotelian philosophy though also influenced by Platonic thought in certain areas. His

---

[1] Julius Guttman, *The Philosophy of Judaism* (Northvale: Jason Aronson Inc., 1988), 120.

principal work, the *Guide to the Perplexed,* is written to reconcile Jewish faith and its challenges by someone well versed in the philosophical tradition. Consequently, HaLevi and Maimonides hold different attitudes towards philosophy. These differences are found throughout their works, including the nature of prophecy.

Yehuda HaLevi's Views

HaLevi's work, *Kuzari,* while written as an *apologia* for Judaism against Christianity and Islam, also reflects his attitude towards philosophy. For HaLevi, the philosopher is concerned primarily with God's theoretical knowledge, rather the experiential knowledge of God.[2] His critique does not end there, as HaLevi denies the possibility of philosophy in achieving certainty in the metaphysical arena. As Julius Guttman notes, for HaLevi, a principle critique is that they possess only pseudo-knowledge.[3]

---

[2] Steven T. Katz, *Jewish Philosophers* (New York: Block Publishing Company, 1975), 66.

[3] Julius Guttman, *The Philosophy of Judaism* (Northvale: Jason Aronson Inc., 1988), 121.

In contrast to the general views of medieval philosophy that prophecy was a universally accessible experience, HaLevi believed that Israel alone among the nations possessed the gift of prophecy.[4] In the words of a fictional character, the Kuzari, HaLevi reveals a slight towards the philosophical tradition.

> "Moreover, one might expect the gift of prophecy to be quite common among philosophers, considering their deeds, their knowledge, their researches after truth, their exertions and their close connection with all things spiritual; one might expect that wonders, miracles, and extraordinary things would be reported of them. Yet we find that true visions are granted to persons who do not devote themselves to study or the purification of

---

[4] Steven T. Katz, *Jewish Philosophers* (New York: Block Publishing Company, 1975), 66. "For me it is sufficient that God chose them as His community and people from all the nations of the world; that the Divine power descended on the whole people, so that they all became worthy to be addressed by Him. The power even swayed their women, among whome were prophetess. Up to that time the power had descended from Adam isolated individuals only." Hans Lewy, Alexander Altmann, and Isaak Heinemann, *3 Jewish Philosophers* (New York: Meridian Books, Inc, 1960), 45.

their souls. This proves that between the Divine power and the soul, there are secret relations which are not identical with those thou mentioned, O Philosopher!"[5]

For HaLevi, direct religious experience it superior to deductive reasoning. For HaLevi, the prophet is one who, by an inner sense, is able to comprehend spiritual reality. The prophet experiences the presence of God directly.[6] As Katz notes:

"The prophetic faculty is a faculty beyond ordinary human reason, and constitutes a generic distinction between the prophet and the ordinary man, parallel to the distinction between man and animals."[7]

The prophet does not teach men eternal truths, but rather the path of observance that leads men to God's presence.

---

[5] Hans Lewy, Alexander Altmann, and Isaak Heinemann, *3 Jewish Philosophers* (New York: Meridian Books, Inc, 1960), 30.
[6] Steven T. Katz, *Jewish Philosophers* (New York: Block Publishing Company, 1975), 68.
[7] Ibid. 68.

Unlike most Jewish philosophers of the medieval period and certainly Maimonides, HaLevi is not concerned with any inconsistencies between Jewish tradition and philosophical tradition or reconciling them. HaLevi does not reproach philosophical inquiry because he does not credit them with either scientific or religious discovery. As Isaak Heinemann notes in his review of HaLevi's approach to philosophy: " How can the Greeks be expected to be in full possession of the truth!"[8]

Through the person of the Rabbi in the Kuzari, HaLevi states:

"These are some of the characteristics of the undoubted prophet. Through him, God made manifest to the people that He is in connection with them, that there is a LORD who guides them as

---

[8] Hans Lewy, Alexander Altmann, and Isaak Heinemann, *3 Jewish Philosophers* (New York: Meridian Books, Inc, 1960), 55.

He wishes, according to their obedience or disobedience."[9]

For HaLevi, the prophet's role and the distinction of Israel are based upon the historical revelation at Sinai and in the sign and miracles that the God of Abraham, Isaac, and Israel performed for their children in Egypt.[10] The source of religious truth is biblical revelation, whose veracity is based upon the revelation's public nature.[11]

---

[9] Hans Lewy, Alexander Altmann, and Isaak Heinemann, *3 Jewish Philosophers* (New York: Meridian Books, Inc, 1960), 37.

[10] Kuzari, Book 1:12. HaLevi emphasizes the "historicity" of the revelation by stating "But the facts are yet more startling. The Israelites lived Egypt as slaves, 600,000 men above the age of twenty, the descendants of the Twelve Tribes…All these plaques were preceded by warnings… and their cessation was signalled in the same way, proving that they were ordained by God, who does what He wills and when He wills, and that they are not ordinary natural phenomena." Hans Lewy, Alexander Altmann, and Isaak Heinemann, *3 Jewish Philosophers* (New York: Meridian Books, Inc, 1960), 42.

[11] Julius Guttman, *The Philosophy of Judaism* (Northvale: Jason Aronson Inc., 1988), 120.

The Views of Maimonides

Despite the enormous accomplishments of Maimonides in the area of Jewish law, the collection and classification of Jewish law in his *Mishneh Torah* serves to reveal but a bit of Maimonides' review of Judaism through the heavily influenced scope of Aristotelian philosophy.

In his *Guide to the Perplexed,* Maimonides reveals his views regarding achieving real knowledge of God. He tells the story of a king and his palace surrounded by his realm. His subjects are scattered throughout his dominions, some closer than others. Those closer to the palace reflect a deeper connection to God. Yet, even within the palace, there are differences in the quality of knowledge they hold.

> "Those who arrive at the palace but go round about it, are those who devote themselves exclusively to the study of the practical law; they believe traditionally in true principles of faith and learn the practical worship of God, but are not trained in the philosophical treatment of the

principles of the Law…Those who undertake to investigate the principles of religion have come into the ante-chamber…But those who have succeeded in finding a proof for everything that can be proved, who have a true knowledge of God, so far as a true knowledge can be attained, and are near the truth, wherever an approach to the truth is possible, they have reached the goal, and are in the palace in which the king lives…when you understand Physics, you have entered the hall; and when, after completing the study of Natural Philosophy, you master Metaphysics, you have entered the innermost court, and are with the king in the same palace. You have attained the degree of the wise men…"[12]

---

[12] M. Friedlander, trans., *The Guide for the Perplexed* (New York: Dover, 1956), 385.

For Maimonides, truth is universal. This accessibility to all mankind reveals how Abraham came to the knowledge of God. According to Midrashic texts, Abraham, through his speculation, concluded that idols are not God. Abram, a Gentile, becomes the first Jew through philosophical speculation. Abraham is the first to reason the existence of the one true God.

In connection with this view on the universality of truth is his views on prophecy. Maimonides accepts the philosophers' view that prophecy is a particular faculty of man that reaches a perfection state.[13] It is accessible to all, though few develop this "trait." Prophecy is brought about only by a state of perfection. Maimonides states:

> "But if a person, perfect in his intellectual and moral faculties, and also perfect, as far as possible, in his imaginative faculty, prepares himself in the manner which will be described, he must become

---

[13] Ibid., 219.

a prophet; for prophecy is a natural faculty of man."[14]

This view sharply differs from HaLevi, who viewed prophecy as an immediate communion between God and man. He also objected to it on the nature of religious relationships, which he argued were initiated by God alone.[15] Commenting on HaLevi, Guttman states:

> "All of them [philosophy and various religions] seek to attain communion with God, but as long as they endeavor to discover the means thereto by themselves, they never get beyond the illusion of such a communion."[16]

His authorship of the *Thirteen Principles* of Jewish faith as a definitive summary of the essence of Judaism reveals Maimonides' thinking about Judaism via a

---

[14] Ibid., 220.
[15] Julius Guttman, *The Philosophy of Judaism* (Northvale: Jason Aronson Inc., 1988), 124.
[16] Ibid., 124.

philosophical site. Maimonides includes the existence of God, His unity, His incorporeality, and His eternity.[17]

Maimonides creed then is based upon the same philosophical approach as Aristotle. The Supreme Being's unchanging qualities, immutable nature, and the articulation of God as ultimate perfection do not reflect the biblical and classical rabbinic view of describing God through His acts on behalf of Israel. The Exodus from Egypt, the splitting of the Sea of Reeds, the revelation at Sinai are the events through which Judaism understands God.[18] The generalizations of Aristotelian thought adopted by Maimonides regarding God's goodness or His perfection or the essence of His being diverged from the Biblical picture of God's character revealed in specific instances for specific people. The God of Israel is not known through the pure contemplation of the Divine

---

[17] Heschel comments that Maimonides' creed is based on the premise that ultimate reality is realized in the ideas. Abraham Joshua Heschel, *God in Search of Man: A Philosophy of Judaism* (New York: JPS, 1955), 21.

[18] Abraham Joshua Heschel, *God in Search of Man: A Philosophy of Judaism* (New York: JPS, 1955), 20-21.

nature but in recognizing and awareness of His historic and ongoing acts of kindness.

Maimonides is preoccupied with the ever-present challenge of the Bible's anthropomorphic description of God, His incorporeality, and a proper understanding of God's essence. Maimonides states:

> "It will be explained later that those who possess a *true knowledge* of God do not consider that He possesses many attributes but believe that these various attributes which describe His Might, Greatness, Power, Perfection, Goodness, etc. are identical, denoting *His Essence*, and not anything extraneous to *His Essence*."[19]

In Aristotelian thought, God is the perfect being. Thinking or contemplation is the perfect thing for a philosopher. Then God must spend all of his time thinking. What does he think about? He must think about perfect

---

[19] On the Homonyms in the Bible Chapter XX M. Friedlander, Moses Maimonides, *The Guide for the Perplexed* (New York: Dover Press, 1956), 29.

things. Since he is the only perfect thing, he must think about himself, or else imperfect thoughts enter his mind. Perfection is to be static. For God to retain his perfection, he cannot change. He cannot have any relationships with imperfect beings. In the end, this view provides the most significant contrast between the opinions of HaLevi and Aristotelian philosophers like Maimonides. Guttman writes:

> "Thus, Judah HaLevi is enabled to place philosophy as mere knowledge of God, in fundamental opposition to religion, which is life with God. The pious man is driven to God not by a desire for knowledge, but by his yearning for communion with him…the yearning heart seeks the God of Abraham; the labor of the intellect is directed toward the God of Aristotle."[20]

---

[20] Julius Guttman, *The Philosophy of Judaism* (Northvale: Jason Aronson Inc., 1988), 125.

CHAPTER 8

Accommodation or Particularistic Approaches

Modern Jewish movements, i.e., Reform, Conservative, Political, etc., came into being out of the desire and need of Jewish communities to address the challenge of living in two competing civilizations at the same time. Ashkenazic Jewry was particularly faced with this challenge; their Sephardic and Italian counterparts faced the same challenge, albeit in different political and social circumstances. However, Modernity's challenge is reflective of the age-old confrontation Jews have faced since the inception of Israelite peoplehood.

In the aftermath of the destruction of the Second Temple and the near-complete exodus of Jews from Israel's land, Jewish exposure to and confrontation with non-Jewish life and philosophy increased. Jews particularly felt this challenge in the medieval period living in Christian and Islamic civilizations, where Jews found themselves the primary minority.

The Particularistic Approach

Various approaches to deal with different world views consequently developed within the Jewish community and remain today. The first approach regarding interaction with the outside world is the so-called Particularistic position that embraces the view that Jewish thinking has its own native categories; other non-Jewish thinking modes are superfluous or even damaging to Jewish thought and authenticity. It has also been referred to as the "way of insulation" by David Hartman. At its extreme, the "way of insulation" approach, as Hartman describes, simply rejects and dismisses "foreign modes of thought" by refusing to accept them as serious.

Attempting to explain or substantiate Jewish values within the category of another philosophical or religious framework requires affirming the competing system as rational and legitimate to some extent. If one denies outside views as inherently lacking any legitimate claim, one only needs to ignore it.[1]

This position's strength and advantage are its very insulation and protection of an entire body of knowledge from all severe challenges. Problematic questions are simply denied legitimacy. The ultimate guarantor of real knowledge is found in God, as the ultimate source of revelation. With God as the guarantor of true knowledge, any competing claim is easily dismissed; moreover, considering alternative foreign claims or philosophies hints of irrationality and arrogance.[2] The act of dedicating oneself to a manner of life decreed by God automatically delegitimizes any claim made by human reason independently made without divine revelation.

---

[1] David Hartman, *Maimonides: Torah and Philosophic Quest* (Philadelphia: Jewish Publication Society, 1976), 8.
[2] Ibid., 9.

This view is found in the 12th and 13th centuries in response to the rise of Jewish philosophy but was also espoused by rabbis of the Renaissance period. For Judah Loew of Prague, Judaism can only be expressed in its own native terms. For Judah Loew, Maimonides was poisoned through his exposure to foreign influences since the study of philosophy lent legitimacy to outside knowledge. For the Maharal, truth does not exist outside of Judaism.[3]

Interestingly, while opposing philosophical inquiry, the Maharal embraced Kabalistic thought, which was strongly influenced by Platonic ideas. Judah Loew of Prague argued that *Kabbalah* is an authentic way of Jewish thinking, and philosophy is not. To justify his acceptance of Kabbalah, Judah Loew of Prague argued that the word Kabbalah comes from the word *kibel,* meaning tradition. That is, Kabbalah is the mesorah. In

---

[3] Interestingly Dr. Sherwin argues that without believing that Judaism is better than other religious ideas, Jews will not adhere to Judaism. Judaism has to be viewed as superior – an idea I whole heartedly embrace.

contrast, "Jewish philosophy" is never referred to as the tradition or as *kibel*. Philosophy is instead the individual contemplation of the philosopher. For the Maharal, it is based on Greek thinking, which has several claims inimical to Jewish life. The Maharal also pointed to the pseudo work entitled *Tefilato sh'Aristo* - The Prayer of Aristotle in which Aristotle repents and asks God for forgiveness for introducing ideas that were inimical to Judaism to buttress his attack on philosophical inquiry. For Judah Lowe, authentic Jewish philosophy is Jewish thinking. As a result, the Maharal attacked Gershonides and Maimonides as embracing non-Jewish forms of Jewish thought.

Rabbi Moses Isserles, however, argued against the Maharal's vehement opposition to all philosophical inquiry and can be viewed as a reconciler between philosophical inquiry and mysticism. For Rabbi Isserles, there was no real clash between philosophy and mysticism. They are both a part of the tradition because they are the same thing, but they speak about things in different ways, and hence both are legitimate ways of Jewish thinking.

For Rabbi Isserles, Plato and the other Greek philosophers derived their knowledge from Jewish sources. He argued that the Jews invented philosophy and went as far as to assert that Plato was a disciple of King David and Solomon. His assertion considered how the Greeks espoused views inimical to Jewish thought and why philosophy had fallen out of favor in Jewish circles. Moreover, Jews did not know philosophy because of the tribulations of Jewish life. According to Isserles, the Greeks learned philosophy but corrupted it by introducing various ideas that deviated from its Jewish foundations. As far as Isserles was concerned, the task of Jews was to reconstruct philosophy as it was initially.

The Accomodationist Approach

The alternative to the Particularistic approach is the Accomodationist approach. The accommodationist position's basis lies in the confrontation, exposure, and finally, engagement with non-Jewish forms of thinking and life. At one extreme, this approach includes a dualistic approach that reflects a continuing loyalty to one's tradition while accepting the truth-claims of a competing system. At its extreme, the dualistic approach separates an individual's knowledge from his practices. In this mode, the individual can disregard the outer forms of observances as merely contributing to the well being of a well-ordered community. Rituals and traditions can be viewed as meaningless. Still, the moral actions justify the spurious claims upon which the former are based.[4] The dualistic approach protects the tradition from counterclaims. It bifurcates the realms of thought and action. As Hartman notes, "the god of metaphysics and the god of history are never confused." A person's acquiescence to this kind of thinking and its theological claims are justified by the inherent functionality it affords rather than by the truth it claims.[5]

---

[4] David Hartman, *Maimonides: Torah and Philosophic Quest* (Philadelphia: Jewish Publication Society, 1976), 10.
[5] Ibid., 10, 12.

The accomodationist approach can also be viewed as a way of integration. An individual does not have to approach faith and reason as an either/ or approach. The individual takes the knowledge claims of outside sources seriously but allows for the validity of human thought to engage him. For the integrationist, Divine revelation need not conflict with human understanding. But when human understanding appears to conflict with a traditional understanding of religious tradition, the integrationist allows for rational truth to alter religious texts' literal meaning. The integrationist allows for the supremacy of the knowledge of God. Still, it recognizes the endowment of Creation by God with reason.[6]

Saadia Gaon: The First Medieval Accomodationists

A primary example of the accomodationist view is Saadia Gaon. He was born in Egypt and studied in Babylonia in Sura and Pumbedita, where he eventually served

---

[6] Ibid., 15, 17.

as the Gaon of both communities. The lists of his accomplishments are varied, include the first to translate the Bible into Arabic, the first codification of the Jewish Prayer book, and the first Hebrew grammar. He is considered the Father of medieval Jewish philosophy and believed it was possible to reach the same truth as found in Jewish faith by applying reason. For Saadia, the truth found in the body of Jewish writings reflects divine revelation. Philosophical truth must be the same. Saadia's assertion, however, raises the question as to why Jewish tradition is important and relevant.

Saadia presented two answers as a response. Saadia argued that many people could not learn to apply reason to discover the truth since it would take a significant amount of time to deduct such essential truths. If, for example, society did not regard stealing as wrong except through the process of divine revelation, it would not have sufficient time to discover this truth. Revelation and tradition, therefore, accelerate the learning process.[7]

---

[7] Rabbi Eliezer Ashkenazi was a Sephardic rabbi who was an extreme rationalist who eventually resided in Krakow in the 16th

For Saadia, a faith-based on reasoned analysis and existential experience is a stronger faith. As St. Anselm of Canterbury, a contemporary of Saadia, noted, "Our goal is to understand what we already believe."

A critical concern for Saadia in his apologetics was the existence of the predominant religion since the prominent religion has distinct advantages in any debate. Since the Moslems embraced the rules of philosophy as a legitimate framework for debate, those, in turn, were necessarily the ground rules for any religious debate. But while using the same levels, the playing field to a certain extent when dealing with polemics certainly makes sense, one can undoubtedly question if it betters Jewish self-understanding and whether these methods should be used to explain the Jewish community to the outside.

---

century. He wrote *Sefer Maaseh Hashem* in which he asked how did Abraham come to the knowledge of God. He doubted everything and then reconstructed everything until he proved the existence of God. Rational truth is Truth and religious truth must be understood in this context.

The Accomodationists of Medieval Spain

While the Diaspora's realities had positioned Jews as minorities in all cultures for much of Jewish history, the influence, exposure, and opportunity to engage non-Jewish forms of thinking varied. During the golden age of Jewry in Spain, wealthy Spanish Jews were mainly drawn by outside influences. Exposed to the intellectual renaissance occurring during Islamic rule and the rediscovery of classical Greek texts, they were convinced that there were other routes to God, so much so that according to later popular belief in the post expulsion period, they were expelled from Spain as a result of their waywardness and infidelity to the singularity and uniqueness of Jewish thought.

Interestingly, comparisons between then day Spanish Jewry and the modern Jewish community can be made. Today, Jewish communities often seek to define spirituality by extra -Jewish modes and replace the mitzvoth as the cornerstone of Jewish identity, thought, and practice. In short, this superfluous approach to Jewish thought simply views foreign modes of thought as simply reflecting many components already found in Jewish thought.

Those ideas outside of Jewish thought, seen as strengthening the Jewish experience, were and are included. Theoretically, those dangerous to the community are rejected. An example of this is a Hasid who brings a popular peasant tune into the synagogue and incorporates it into the synagogue service, thereby "sanctifying" it to a higher level. Another example is that of the *Takanah* of Rabbenu Gershom, which instituted monogamy among Jews. When it was promulgated, his contemporary rabbis, especially Sephardic ones, challenged this because it was influenced by *Chukat haGoy*, (i.e., that is the way of the Gentiles). Nonetheless, the practice has remained, though he derived this from Christian standards of his day.

The Accomodationist Position in the Medieval Period

In the 13th and 14th centuries, there was considerable controversy over Maimonides and his philosophical inquiry and speculation. This debate continued even after the expulsion from Spain. Debates continued as to whether foreign ideas could be introduced to the circle of Jewish thought.

In the medieval period, the law of exclusion was adopted: "It is true or untrue." For philosophers who argued that philosophy is true and the Torah is also true, the two's relationship had to be established. It was determined that one of the two must be false, or both must be true because they, in fact, reflected the same ideas. This became the great enterprise of Jewish thinkers to show that Christian and Jewish thought were mainly the same. The religious texts and philosophical texts were viewed as essentially saying the same thing. This became the enterprise of philosophical theology, which was based on the proposition that the claims of philosophical inquiry and religious tradition were the same – hence the "The Double faith Theory." They are necessarily the same in content, though perhaps not methodology.

The accomodationist position at its height is seen in the views of Maimonides. For Maimonides, the views in certain Biblical verses correlated to certain philosophical concepts. Anthropomorphic ideas were to be rejected. God is the Aristotelian idea of God. He truly believed the Bible was in harmony with Aristotelian philosophy.[8] In the end, Maimonides sides with Jewish faith regarding the Creation of the world.

---

[8] Kabalistic ideas were accepted within the tradition and were not seen as a threat and were not a threat to the observance structure and strengthened the observance structure in contrast to Maimonides whose philosophical views could be taken to justify observance of the mitzvoth. Among the mystics there was an upsurge in observance like the steak that is eaten and assimilated. Kabalist thought did not identify its ideas as Platonic in origin.

The medieval period saw Levi ben Gershon author the work *Sefer Milmahot Hashem*. It was debated intensely and dubbed *the wars against God* by its critics. For Saadia, rational truth and religious truth are the same. When there is a conflict between religious and rational truth, rational truth wins. Sherwin argues that this is the pigmy approach to Jewish self-understanding. For Gersonides, there is truth in Judaism, but there is greater truth outside. This reflects one end of the accomodationist perspective. The ultimate transcendent truth surpasses the individualistic truths of particular religions. For Judah Loew of Prague, Judaism can only be expressed in its own native terms. For Maimonides and Saadia, there are truths outside of Judaism, but Judaism is definitive in the end.

18th Century Accomodationism

The Jewish Emancipation of the 18th century and the Enlightenment (i.e., the bicultural option) became a key feature of Jewish life. They were brought into interaction with the accomodationist view.

Moses Mendelssohn was the first great Jewish German philosopher of the period. For Mendelssohn, as well as his non-Jewish contemporaries, rational truth is absolute. As the medieval philosophers said, it must be valid for all places and all people. Judaism, if it claims to be valid, must be universally true. Since the assertions of Christianity are rational, they must be true as well. The rationality of Jewish practices was scrutinized.

As a result of this rationalist trend, the early Reformers revised and shortened the liturgy Mystical and emotional elements were deleted. The traditional rabbinic job description was made obsolete since the binding nature of the law was changed. The Rabbi's role should be pastoral rather than legal. Halakhah had been the unifying force in the past in light of persecution, a view proposed first by Spinoza. With Emancipation, reason dictated that since there was no persecution, the law was no longer required. Theology and ethics replaced halakhah as the unifying force. The Reforms emphasized the Bible as the central piece of sacred literature. Talmud and Patristic literature both corrupted their respective religions. As far as the Reformers were concerned, Luther and the reformers rejected the concept of sacred language. Certain Reformers went as far as to argue that German was a sacred language, even in America.

The desire to review Judaism through a rational prism was further advanced by using non-Jewish historical and critical approaches by Jews reached its height in Germany with the adoption of *Wissenschaft des Judentums* - the scientific study of Jewish texts and Judaism. According to Dr. Sherwin, it was embraced because scientific research did the same thing as Saadiah's embracement of philosophy. If everyone used the same methods, this equalized the "playing field" of argumentation between Judaism and Christianity and could be used to scientifically show that Jews should be granted acceptance and equal rights within European society.[9]

In Reform Jewish circles, the essence was desired while the tangential could be eliminated. Zunz concluded the Reformers had gone too far! One of these issues was circumcision. The Reformers argued that circumcision was tangential and barbaric. Zunz argued that this was too far. You can take out Hebrew, peoplehood, etc. History becomes the judge of Jewish thinking instead of Jewish sacred texts.

---

[9] History became the central concern of the German Jewish school. Everything including theology, Talmud, the Bible etc are reviewed by history. In Europe, Wissenshaft was used construct a certain portrait of Judaism. One example of its use is a case in which Prussia made a law that Jews had to have Jewish names. Leopold Zunz was asked by the Jewish community about this law. He wrote a monograph on the subject that Jews throughout history always used non Jewish names. On this basis the Prussian government rescinded the law. Leo Baeck a great Jewish leader who refused to leave Germany in the midst of Nazi's rise to power argued that Wissenshaft was a failure and that it reduced all to history eclipsing the theology and history behind it. Historically, there has not been much emphasis on history from Jewish theological perspectives, but rather that Jewish theology influenced how history was understood.

Julius Wellhausen was the founder of the critical historical approach to the Bible and the Documentary Hypothesis. He questioned what the essence of Christianity was. He argued that the essence of Judaism was ethical monotheism, as reflected in the later prophets. He argues that Jesus embraced the prophetic version of Judaism. Right-wing Protestantism, rabbinic Judaism, etc. were attempts to distort this ethical monotheism.

The early Reformers followed Wellhausen's view. For the Reformers, the Law was not necessary, rather the "universalistic moral teachings," which were common to both Judaism and Christianity. Margolis argued that the Bible was the common element between Jews and Christians. Judaism is not an alien civilization but at the heart and core of the American and western experience. One of the manifestations of the accomodationist mode is the emergence of Jewish philosophical responses. This can easily wind up with the double sources of truth.

Mendelssohn is the first "Modern Jew" is on the scene when the bicultural option is viable. Religious truth is rational by nature. Judaism is a rational religion. Religion, to be true, must come to the same essential beliefs. They only differ based on custom practice etc. Mendelssohn had a Christian friend name, Lavater. In one of those events, Mendelssohn beat Kant in one of those philosophical debates. One day, Lavater wrote Mendelssohn and asked if Judaism and Christianity were necessarily the same, then why not convert. Within 100 years, all of Mendelssohn's descendants were Christians.

Am I an Accomodationist or Particularistic?

My position on the matter of accomodationist and particularistic approaches to Jewish thinking is like so many of the Jewish thinkers and philosophers I have read, i.e., rather complicated. There is vibrancy unequaled that I find, for example, in the Bible that surpasses any intellectual inquiry or exercise I am familiar with in philosophy or belief to be in any other religious tradition. To read the words of David that "the Lord is close to those who call upon him," or "Seek the favor of the Lord, and He will give you the desires of your heart" is something which I believe can only be understood from a distinctly Jewish world view.

To know, as Abraham Joshua Heschel stated, that the kindness of the God of Israel *happens* instead of merely being an abstract idea convinces me of the superiority of Israel's God and the unique revelation of God to Israel. The God of Abraham, of Isaac, and of Jacob is not the same as the gods of other traditions as Isaiah notes God speaking, "I am the first, and I am the last, and there is no god but me, who like me can announce, can foretell it- and match me thereby?" [10]

Deuteronomy 4:6 states:

> "For this is your wisdom and your understanding in the sight of the nations which shall hear all these statutes and say, "Surely, that great nation is a wise and discerning people."

---

[10] Isaiah 44:6-8.

Yet as much as I believe with perfect faith (to quote Maimonides) in the superiority of Jewish thought in a particularistic mode, there are certain aspects of, for example, Maimonides writings regarding philosophy that ring strikingly loud.

In my study of *Moreh Nevuchim*, Maimonides appears to regard philosophy as an intellectual love of God, which in many ways exists independently, though certainly not inimically to the Torah. He also tells a story, if I remember correctly, of a castle and the people outside and within. The people outside the castle working and looking away from the castle are like individuals who are busy with everyday life and are not concerned with the castle or its king. The closer one reaches the castle, one finds people who are more cognizant of the king and much more dedicated to his service. There are inner chambers within the castle within which one finds individuals who commune with the king and eat at his table. Maimonides describes each of these groups and connects to religious parallels in the Jewish community. Perhaps the most surprising is the description of one group undoubtedly concerned with the king's service in their actions but goes round and round about the castle without actually entering it. He likens them to those engrossed in halakhah but implies that they miss an aspect of connection to God. For Maimonides, it is philosophy or the intellectual love of God that provides the link for the individual, allowing him to enter into the inner court. If I have understood Maimonides correctly, even those knowledge in the Torah, even great *hachamim,* can lose a connectedness to God.

It seems clear to me that plenty of Jews find resonance with this view. That fact that so many Jews seek Enlightenment or "spirituality" in non-Jewish sources reveals that they feel a route to God necessary apart from their Jewish experience. However, I believe that many "foreign" elements or ideas adopted by "wandering Jews" are elements found within Judaism itself. Because of various circumstances, they have not been cultivated or have been forgotten. The prophet Jeremiah states:

"Thus said the Lord; Stand by the roads and consider, inquire about ancient paths; which is the road to happiness? Travel it and find tranquility for yourselves."[11]

In my opinion, the ancient paths are the wells and superiority of Jewish thought.

---

[11] Jeremiah 6:16.

Glossary of Relevant Terms

Hebrew (Heb); Yiddish (Yid); English (Eng)

Bet HaMikdash (Heb)- "The Sanctified House." The rabbinic term used to refer to the first and second Temples constructed in Jerusalem.

B'nai Israel (Heb)- The children of Israel; i.e., the Jewish people.

Halakhah (Heb)- the collective body of Jewish law. It is derived from the Hebrew word *halakh*, meaning to walk. The implication is that Halakhah shows the Jew which "way he or she should walk" to live in conformity to God's laws.

Kabbalat Mitzvot (Heb) – The acceptance of the commandments. It is used in reference to an aspiring convert accepting the "yoke" of the commandments.

Ketuvim (Heb)- "Writings." The word is derived from the Hebrew from *ktav*, meaning written. It includes all the books of the Hebrew Bible that are not part of the Torah or part of the prophetic books.

Nevi'im (Heb)- prophets, derived from the Hebrew word *navi*, meaning prophet and the word *nevuah* meaning prophecy.

Mitzvot (Heb) - The commandments of the Written and Oral Law.

Oral Law - Rabbinic Judaism maintains that the Torah was revealed in Written and Oral form. The written text is comprised of the "Books of Moses," The Oral Torah provides the interpretation and implementation of the commandments outlined in the Written Torah.

Shabbat (Heb)- the Sabbath; the Seventh-day of rest.

Tanakh (Heb)- The Jewish Bible or Hebrew Scriptures. An acronym for Torah/Nevi'im/Ketuvim. The Torah refers to the five books of Moses. The Nevi'im refers to books that are deemed prophetic. Ketuvim relates to the "Writings" which constitute the remaining books not included in the previous two categories.

Talmud (Heb) - A central text of Rabbinic Judaism composed of the Mishnah and its commentary, the Gemara.

Torah (Heb)- means instruction or teaching and refers explicitly to the Five Books of Moses (i.e., Genesis, Exodus, Leviticus, Numbers, and Deuteronomy). It is the foundation of Jewish life and Jewish law.

RECOMMENDED RESOURCES FOR FURTHER STUDY

This book was intended to provide the reader with a brief review of Jewish identity. To obtain a deeper understanding of Jewish thought, some excellent resources are available. The books below are a few of the many resources that have been published on this subject.

William Barret, *Irrational Man: A Study in Existential Philosophy* (New York: Double Day, 1958).

Thorleif Boman, *Hebrew Thought Compared with Greek* (New York: W.W. Norton & Company, 1960).

Israel I. Efros, *Ancient Jewish Philosophy* (Detroit: Wayne University, 1964).

Michael Wyschogrod, *The Body of Faith: God and the People of Israel* (Northvale: Aaronson, 1996).

Susan A. Handelman, *The Slayer of Moses: The Emergence of Rabbinic Interpretation in Modern Literary Theory* (Albany: State University of New York Press)

Max Kadushin, *A Conceptual Approach to the Mekilta* (New York: Jewish Theological Seminary, 1969)

Max Kadushin, *Organic Thinking: A Study in Rabbinic Thought* (New York: Jewish Theological Seminary, 1938).

Abraham Joshua Heschel, *Moral Grandeur and Spiritual Audacity* (New York: Macmillan, 1997).

Abraham Joshua Heschel, *God in Search of Man: A Philosophy of Judaism* (New York: JPS, 1955).

Moses Maimonides, *The Guide for the Perplexed* (New York: Dover Press, 1956).

Jacob Neusner, *Jews and Christians: The Myth of a Common Tradition* (Eugene: Wipf and Stock Publishers, 1991).

Jacob Neusner, *Judaism as Philosophy, The Method and Message of the Mishnah* (Baltimore: The Johns Hopkins University Press, 1991).

Solomon Schecter, *Aspects of Rabbinic Theology: Major Concepts of the Talmud* (New York: Schocken Books, 1961).

Byron L. Sherwin, *Towards a Jewish Theology* (Lewiston: Edwin Mellen Press: 1991).

H.L. Strack and Gunter Stemberger, *Introduction to the Talmud and Midrash* (Minneapolis: Fortress Press, 1996).

Index

Abraham Joshua Heschel, 30
Aristotle, 12
Blaise Pascal, 9
Israel I. Efros, 22
Judah Loew, 36
Max Kadushin, 42

Michael Wyschogrod, 10
Moses ben Maimon, 14
Philo, 14
Plato, 12
Socrates, 12
Thorleif Boman, 16

ABOUT THE AUTHOR

Rabbi Juan Marcos Bejarano Gutierrez is a graduate of the University of Texas at Dallas. He earned a bachelor of science in electrical engineering. He studied at the Siegal College of Judaic Studies in Cleveland. He received a Master of Arts Degree in Judaic Studies. He completed his doctoral studies at the Spertus Institute in Chicago in 2015. He studied at the American Seminary for Contemporary Judaism and received rabbinic ordination in 2011 from Yeshiva Mesilat Yesharim.

Rabbi Bejarano Gutierrez was a board member of the Society for Crypto-Judaic Studies from 2011-2013. He has published various articles in *HaLapid, The Journal for Spanish, Portuguese and Italian Crypto-Jews*, and *Apuntes-Theological Reflections from a Hispanic-Latino Context*, and is the author of *What is Kosher?* and *What is Jewish Prayer?* He is currently the director of the B'nai Anusim Center for Education at CryptoJewishEducation.com.

If you have enjoyed this book or others that are part of this series, please consider leaving a positive review on Amazon or Goodreads. A positive review helps spread the word and encourages others to study and learn something new.

Printed in Great Britain
by Amazon